✔ W9-CEX-070

Maple Trees

by Marcia S. Freeman

Consulting Editor:
Gail Saunders-Smith, Ph.D.

Consultant:
Jeff Gillman, Associate Professor
of Nursery Management,
University of Minnesota

Pebble Books

an imprint of Capstone Press
Mankato, Minnesota

Pebble Books are published by Capstone Press
1710 Roe Crest Drive, North Mankato, Minnesota 56003
www.capstonepub.com

Library of Congress Cataloging-in-Publication Data
Freeman, Marcia S. (Marcia Sheehan), 1937–
    Maple trees / by Marcia S. Freeman.
    p. cm.—(Trees)
    Includes bibliographical references and index.
    Summary: Simple text and photographs describes the trunks, branches, leaves,
seeds, and life cycle of maple trees.
    ISBN-13: 978-0-7368-0092-1 (hardcover)
    ISBN-13: 978-0-7368-8093-0 (softcover pbk.)
    1. Maple—Juvenile literature. [1. Maple. 2. Trees.] I. Title. II. Series: Trees
(Mankato, Minn.)
QK495.A17F74   1999
583.78′—dc21   98-18294
                                                                          CIP
                                                                           AC

Note to Parents and Teachers

Books in this series may be used together in comparative activities to
investigate different types of trees. This series supports national science
standards for units on the diversity and unity of plant life. This book
describes and illustrates the parts of maple trees. The photographs support
early readers in understanding the text. This book introduces early readers
to vocabulary used in this subject area. The vocabulary is defined in the
Words to Know section. Early readers may need assistance in reading some
words and in using the Table of Contents, Words to Know, Read More,
Internet Sites, and Index/Word List sections of the book.

Printed in the United States of America in Stevens Point, Wisconsin.
082013   007666R

Table of Contents

Maple trees are tall trees.

A maple tree has smooth or rough bark. The bark is gray or brown.

A maple tree has many branches. The branches grow from the trunk.

Maple leaves grow during spring. Maple leaves can be green or red.

Maple leaves have three or five points. The leaves grow across from each other on branches.

14

Maple leaves change colors during autumn. They turn red, yellow, or orange. The leaves fall from a tree during autumn.

16

A maple tree grows small flowers. Seeds grow in flowers. The seeds are called samaras.

Samaras grow in pairs. They fall from a tree during spring or autumn.

20

You can tell a maple
tree by its leaves
and samaras.

Words to Know

bark—the hard covering on the outside of a tree

branch—a part of a tree that grows out of a tree's trunk

flower—the colored part of a plant that makes seeds or fruit

leaf—a flat part of a tree that grows out from a branch

maple—a type of tree that has leaves with three or five points and seeds called samaras

rough—having bumps and dents

samara—a seed of a maple tree; samaras grow in pairs from a flower.

seed—the part of a plant from which a new plant can grow

smooth—being even and flat

trunk—the main stem of a tree

Read More

Gamlin, Linda. Trees. Eyewitness Explorers. New York: Dorling Kindersley, 1993.

Greenaway, Theresa. Trees. Pockets. New York: Dorling Kindersley, 1995.

Internet Sites

FactHound offers a safe, fun way to find Internet sites related to this book. All of the sites on FactHound have been researched by our staff.

Here's all you do:

Visit *www.facthound.com*

FactHound will fetch the best sites for you!

Index/Word List

Word Count: 118
Early-Intervention Level: 13

Editorial Credits
Martha E. Hillman, editor; Clay Schotzko/Icon Productions, cover designer;
    Sheri Gosewisch, photo researcher

Photo Credits
Chuck Place, cover
Dembinsky Photo Assoc. Inc./Randall B. Henne, 6; Adam Jones, 16;
    Mark A. Schneider, 18
Elizabeth Delaney, 10
Ingrid Wood, 20
John Serrao, 4
Nature's Light/William Manning, 1
Rainbow/Bill Binzen, 14
Robert McCaw, 8
William H. Allen Jr., 12